reading in the business education classroom

reading in the business education classroom

by
Larry Mikulecky
Rita Haugh

Business Education
  Consultant:
Ted W. Ivarie

Series Editor
Alfred J. Ciani

National Education Association
Washington, D.C.

The Authors

Larry Mikulecky is Assistant Professor of Education, School of Education, Indiana University, Bloomington. Dr. Mikulecky is coauthor of *Teaching Reading in Secondary School Content Subjects.*

Rita Haugh is Lecturer, School of Journalism, Indiana University, Bloomington. She was formerly a high school teacher in Kansas City, Kansas.

The Business Education Consultant

Ted W. Ivarie is Dean of the School of Business at Eastern Illinois University, Charleston. Dr. Ivarie is a Past President of the National Business Education Association.

The Advisory Panel

Annelle Bonner, Professor/Chairperson, Department of Business Education, University of Northern Mississippi, Hattiesburg; Pauline A. B. Mosney, Business teacher, Dartmouth High School, North Dartmouth, Massachusetts; John S. Nigro, District Department Head, Business Education, North Haven High School, Connecticut; George R. Phillips, Area Coordinator, Hammonton High School, New Jersey; Jan Wollenhaupt, Business teacher, Bridgewater-Fontanelle High School, Fontanelle, Iowa.

The Series Editor

Dr. Alfred J. Ciani is Associate Professor of Education in the Department of Curriculum and Instruction at the University of Cincinnati, Ohio.

Library of Congress Cataloging in Publication Data

Mikulecky, Larry.
   Reading in business education classes.

   (Reading in the content areas)
   Bibliography: p.
   1. Business education.   2. Reading (Higher education)   I. Haugh, Rita, joint author.
II. Series.   III. Series.
HF1111.M54   658' .007   80-11541
ISBN 0-8106-3208-X

CONTENTS

FOREWORD

Reading in the Business Education Classroom has an unmistakable message that shouts, "The buck stops here!" The authors make it quite clear that anyone involved in education has to be concerned with communication and the communication process. Though communication can involve many aspects (reading, writing, listening, oral skills, and nonverbal skills), this book emphasizes the business teacher's responsibility to help students improve their reading skills (vocabulary development, reading efficiency, and interpretative and evaluative abilities). Educators have long maintained that every teacher is a teacher of English. Today reading specialists are saying that, to a certain degree, every teacher is a teacher of reading.

Mikulecky and Haugh show business teachers that teaching certain levels of reading skills is quite within their capabilities. Many of the suggestions and techniques provided are rooted in psychological principles of learning that were part of every teacher's professional training. Though it would be highly desirable for every content area teacher to attend a formal class in the teaching of reading, this book can serve as guide and tutor. Of course, the book does not claim to be a "complete course" in the teaching of reading in business education classes. No single book can serve in all situations. This is why the authors include an annotated bibliography of suggested readings for further enlightenment and growth.

Business teachers can have a positive effect on the reading skills of secondary school students, since there are more class period enrollments in business education courses than in most other subject areas (science, mathematics, foreign language, fine arts, home economics, and vocational courses). Every citizen must be able to read and interpret business information in order to make sound decisions as a consumer, producer, and citizen/voter. Thus, teachers have the opportunity and the obligation to do what they can to advance each student's reading skills.

Mikulecky and Haugh offer the reader a number of easy, in-class techniques useful in identifying students' reading problems—the first step in "teaching reading." By identifying which students have which reading problems and by determining which reading skills are needed to master a given block of work, the teacher is better able to select appropriate remedial reading techniques for those lacking the required skills. The authors also cover techniques for assessing the distinguishing characteristics of textbooks and supplementary printed materials, and suggest ways to develop student-prepared, multilevel reading materials. Other topics include readability formulas, techniques for improving reading readiness, vocabulary, proofreading skills, and techniques for proper textbook usage.

Lest business teachers fear the responsibility for teaching reading is just one more added requirement in an already crowded day, the authors suggest several ways teachers can "free" themselves from a variety of administrative tasks by arranging for students to perform these tasks. The authors even show how to keep a record of students' reading problems and progress and offer a plan for including a number of short reading/learning activities over a block of time—a process referred to as stranding.

Business teachers must stop shirking their responsibility to help business students become better readers. Toward this goal, business teachers will want to take advantage of formal classroom instruction, participation in "reading development" sessions at professional meetings, and the study of books such as this one as they become available.

Dr. Eugene D. Wyllie
Associate Professor of Business Education
Indiana University

PREFACE

A major problem faces content area teachers at the secondary school level. Students in the elementary grades are taught to read narrative prose, but when they enter high school they are expected to be able to read expository material with little or no preparation. Chances are they have never been taught that the two styles of writing require different reading skills. In effect, they have never been taught how to "change gears" for different styles of writing.

The student in a business education course is faced with two basic types of reading material. The first type is skills oriented—the type found in typewriting and shorthand textbooks. This kind of material requires the student to be proficient in word recognition skills and sound-symbol correspondences. The other type of reading material is concept oriented—the type found in business law and economics textbooks. This material requires students to make generalizations and infer relationships. Too often the business education teacher assumes the student possesses those special reading skills needed to master specific curriculum material. The watchword here is *don't assume.*

Today, the increasing sophistication of business needs and the wider range of students enrolling in business education courses make the task of the business education teacher more complex. A single assignment from a single textbook will not meet the ability level or challenge all the students in any one class. The business education teacher must employ a number of strategies designed to engage student interest and increase student understanding.

In this book Larry Mikulecky and Rita Haugh provide both a rationale and explicit, practical suggestions for the business education teacher. With the help of this text, business educators will be able to show their students how to change gears to meet the special requirements of any type of reading material they encounter.

Alfred J. Ciani
Series Editor

1. RATIONALE FOR READING INSTRUCTION IN BUSINESS EDUCATION CLASSES

"Me teach reading? You've got to be kidding! My job is teaching shorthand and typewriting. If students haven't learned to read by the time they're in high school, there's just no hope for them. We should send them back to sixth grade."

Many teachers agree at least in part with the above comments. But we hope this book demonstrates that business students need to become better readers, capable of using the printed word in different ways in their business education classes.

Many business teachers maintain that students often do poorly in their classes because they are unable to read the textbook. Some teachers have even abandoned the textbook because students could not read it. Other business teachers, however, have discovered ways to help students read the class textbook—and in doing so master the subject.

Two traits in particular characterize business teachers who are able to use tests and other printed materials successfully with their classes. These teachers are observant of their students' accomplishments and realistic about what they can and cannot expect of themselves as teachers. Business teachers whose classes seem to work to the benefit of nearly all students don't structure their classes on the basis of faculty lounge wisdom and gossip, nor do they pretend that today's classroom problems can be solved by blaming others for student deficiencies.

An example is in order. It is not unusual for faculty to post or share a newspaper clipping or article decrying low levels of student literacy. Perhaps a functional illiterate somewhere received a diploma, or a university composition professor is alarmed at the lowered levels of writing ability among high school students, or figures are reported on minimum competency tests.

Such a news clipping always kicks standard replies from those present. One or two may begin with an "ain't it awful" response and end by sharing an anecdote about a particular student's failure. The conversation invariably drifts to the speaker's pet peeve, be it hallway litter, tardiness, or lack of respect.

Usually however, another teacher safely points out that the influence of parents and the home makes the difference, and teachers can't do much about that. An English teacher may break in to underscore the dangers of too much television viewing and not enough novel reading. By the time such a conversation has run its course, drugs, high divorce rates, irresponsible elementary teachers, lack of respect for traditions, and poor eating habits may all be singled out for a share of the blame. As the class bell rings and teachers depart, many feel depressed and helpless. If all these factors are causing the problem, what can one teacher do? Most decide the best course is to cope as best one can and at least maintain some minimum level of standards.

Business education teachers who succeed in using printed materials don't fall into the trap described above. They instinctively realize there is not much to be gained and something to be lost in playing the "who is to blame" game. They may even be aware that many school reading problems stem from the unmet challenge of serving the 10 to 15 percent of the student population who would have dropped out two decades ago. Reading demands have increased at all levels of society. Reading in the business education classroom can present problems because the demands are higher and the student population in these classes has grown and diversified from its original elite corps of students.

Rather than become depressed by "ain't it awful" gossip or the "who's to blame" conversations, the effective business education teacher assesses the problem realistically. As the range of student types in a class broadens, a wider range of abilities must be expected. Blaming elementary teachers is not only counter-productive, it is inaccurate. Elementary student scores in basic beginning reading have actually improved in the last five years. The problem then is not with basic reading but rather with the student's ability to comprehend more difficult textbooks and change gears to meet special reading demands in each content area.

All content area teachers, especially business teachers, must be prepared to teach the special reading and learning skills required of students in their particular content area. Because teachers have mastered their own content area, they often have not stopped to analyze the specialized reading and learning skills students need to demonstrate in their classroom. Many students do not find it easy to understand or retain information from business education textbooks or assigned readings. Students who are taught to refine their business reading skills, acquire information through reading, master content vocabulary, develop interpretive and evaluative reading abilities, and develop positive business attitudes are likely to become mature, effective, and interested readers and users of business materials. Only the most competent students can transfer reading skills from a reading or English class to other classes. The best approach then is to analyze and briefly teach the reading skills most frequently required in the business education class. The person best prepared for this task is the business education teacher.

HOW WIDE IS THE RANGE OF STUDENT ABILITY?

One aspect of school reading difficulties is due to the fact that the high school population now represents a much wider range of student abilities as more students remain for all or part of high school. Many business education teachers had grown accustomed to teaching the "cream of the crop." The expanded enrollment now makes business education students more representative of the total population. The bright students are still in attendance, but they are being joined by higher percentages of average and below average students.

Picture Jane, Tim, and Joe—three typical students in a tenth-grade class in beginning typewriting. Jane, an average student, has a mental age of 16, matching her physical age. Tim, one of the brightest students in the school, has a mental age of 24—for all practical purposes, the mind of an adult. Joe has trouble in school and is thinking about dropping out. His mental age is 11—that of the average fifth grader. So even though this is a "tenth-grade" classroom, the mental age of students spans 13 years, not just one or two! In the secondary school it is not unusual to find an 8 to 12 year range within a single class. Comparable figures exist for both reading ability and computational ability.

Elementary school teachers face the same problem, but on a smaller scale. In the typical first grade classroom, for example, the slowest student may have a mental age of four, the average student an age of six, and the brightest student a mental age of nine. So even in the first grade a range of five years can be seen. The wide range of reading abilities appears to be a permanent spin-off of mandatory public education and campaigns to keep adolescents in school. Better teaching can slightly increase the average ability of a group, but it also tends to increase the ability range even more as bright students race ahead.

The widening range of student ability is also affected, as mentioned earlier, by the increase in the number of students who remain in school. In 1910 only nine percent of 17-year-olds completed high school. In 1940 barely half of the 17-year-olds—51 percent—graduated from high school. Generally, the brightest students stayed in school and those who had the most difficulty left. In 1960 about 65 percent of 17-year-olds completed high school. In 1970 the figure stood at 76 percent.(1) As the percentage of those who stay to finish high school increases, the range of individual differences among students widens.

Few schools have classes with homogeneous students. Even pupils in tracked classes demonstrate a range of ability that spans five to seven years. Students vary not only in mental ability, but also in family background, interests, hobbies, skill in reading and computation, habits of workmanship, attitude, and even in why they chose to take the course. Some students always get good grades; others have never earned a grade higher than a C. Some have good study habits and like to study; others haven't yet learned how to study.

Another sign of the range of reading ability is speed of reading. The amount of time spent on an assignment can vary greatly, depending on the student's reading ability. Kenneth Dulin(2) in examining reading test results, found that tenth graders who were among the least capable readers read only 140 words per minute, while those among the best readers read 359 words or more per minute. So a teacher who assigns the same material to all students in a class can expect the least motivated students to spend more than twice as much time on each assignment. A half-hour assignment for top readers takes slow readers more than an hour to complete. Usually attention and concentration lags long before the hour is up. A poor reader with assignments in several classes may face many more hours of reading than the competent reader.

Students also exhibit wide differences in vocabulary and comprehension levels. Students in an "average" tenth-grade class vary in vocabulary levels from fifth to fifteenth grade (third year in college) and in comprehension levels from fourth grade to college graduate. Accounting teachers using a text with a tenth-grade readability level will find that half their tenth-graders read above tenth-grade level and half read below tenth-grade level. (The student who is at the exact middle or average of the group's ability range is said to be at grade level.) Teachers who say, "Read chapter three for tomorrow," find that without a great deal of in-class preparation, 50 percent of the class won't understand the reading and may not even complete it. Many of the brighter students may complete the reading but be bored by it; some brighter students may simply wait until the next day when the teacher explains the entire assignment to the poorer readers who were unable to read the text.

The problem of readability level is compounded by the fact that some high school texts are more difficult than publishers' claims suggest. Readability studies of secondary school textbooks indicate that some are one to five grades above the average ability of the target audience. If a teacher assigns students to read independently, more than half the average class—perhaps as many as 70 percent—will fail to comprehend the assignment. Some publishers have rewritten textbooks several grade levels below the intended level so that poor readers can be reached.

Obviously this wide range of reading ability poses problems for all subject matter teachers. Poor readers not only spend a disproportionate amount of time on each assignment but also read so slowly that most cannot hold onto ideas and concepts. Even those few textbooks written exactly at grade level will still be too difficult for the lower half of an "average" class and may leave the stu-

dents in the top 20 percent of the class unchallenged. Clearly, the traditional teaching approach of one text and one assignment is not likely to succeed.

Though the problem of illiteracy has received a good deal of attention, many business education teachers must cope with another sort of student. These students seem bright enough, and test scores back this up, but they simply won't read assignments. Though they are able to read, they lack the predisposition toward literacy that students had in the era preceding television. Some reading experts label such students *aliterate*—not illiterate; they are able to read but choose not to do so. Teaching such students is more a problem of motivation than intellect.

Because the use of printed materials can present so many problems, business teachers are wise to set aside some class time early in the semester to identify the particular reading deficiencies of their students and prepare such students for some degree of success in their class. Teachers can lead students to become aware of the appropriate use and value of written language in the business education classroom and later in occupational settings. Time spent early in the semester makes students more competent and helps them comprehend and retain more complex written material introduced later in the semester.

DIFFICULTY OF TEXTS

When students are asked to evaluate their textbooks, terms like "boring," "stupid," or "dull" often head the list of adjectives. Students will sometimes use the same terms to explain why they haven't completed or even attempted to read business education assignments. Often this negative attitude is merely a cover-up for personal inability. Who wants to admit that a textbook is too difficult?

Textbooks fail to hold a student's attention for many reasons: a lack of familiarity with technical words, a lack of a frame of reference from which to work, or impatience with an unfamiliar style.

Business teachers cannot assume that students are interested in the topic and find the reading easy to manage. So teachers must start the school year with the premise that the main text may be "boring and difficult" for many students in the class.

How can teachers review materials before giving them to students? One approach is to use a checklist like the one that follows:

1. *Interest area or type*—What kinds of topics are emphasized?

2. *Inference requirements*—Does the writing style require a large amount or small amount of inference?

3. *Vocabulary*—Is the vocabulary difficult or technical or both?

4. *Organizational aids*—Does the format feature numerous heads or other means to help the reader organize thoughts and guide the movement of ideas?

5. *New concepts*—Do the authors provide sufficient background when explaining new concepts?

6. *Frame of reference*—How distant from students' lives are the examples and tasks in the text?

Another way to determine if a text is appropriate for a class is to use a readability formula. Most readability formulas assume that the more difficult the vocabulary and the longer the sentences, the more difficult the passage. Although these formulas can help a teacher quantify the difficulty of a passage, no formula can measure complexity of ideas or provide an in-depth measure of the student's experiential background, maturity, interest, and purpose for reading.

Readability formulas also fail to identify which students will experience particular difficulty with a text. The cloze technique, developed by Wilson Taylor, has proven effective for determining the match-up between student and text. The cloze technique uses actual passages from the text under consideration to provide a reasonably accurate picture of which students can read the text independently, which can read the text with some teacher aid, and which ought to be reading less difficult material. See Chapter 2 for more information on the cloze technique.

Cloze exercises, readability formulas, and a few carefully constructed early assignments can provide the business education teacher with in-depth information about text difficulty and individual student ability. Such information can help a teacher anticipate problems and avoid a great deal of wasted teaching effort.

THE CHANGING STUDENT POPULATION IN BUSINESS EDUCATION CLASSES

As mentioned earlier, more students are graduating from high school today than ever before in American history. Rather than enter the work force, more students are staying in school longer than ever before. This means that teachers are faced with larger percentages of average and below average students.

Students in business education classes represent a cross-section of the student body, ranging from the unmotivated potential dropout to the motivated, competent college-bound pupil. Because educational leaders encourage everyone to learn to type, more than 70 percent of secondary school students enroll in one to two semesters of typing.(3)

The academic ability of students in different business education classes is not uniform. The typical introductory General Business class usually has average and slightly below average students. Accounting seems to attract average and slightly above average students. Typewriting, like any required English or social studies class, attracts all kinds of students. Shorthand attracts average students below the caliber needed to do well.

A wide and growing variety of students enroll in business education despite the fact that no state requires any business courses. (A few states require that students take a consumerism class.) As a matter of fact, business class enrollment supercedes enrollment in some traditionally required subjects. In Indiana, the greatest total number of students are enrolled in English and social studies courses, which are required; business, an elective, placed third, before science and math, which are also required. Nationally, enrollment in business classes is in fourth or fifth place in the secondary school curriculum.

Enrollment statistics reflect a growing sensitivity to the employment needs of our nation. In a society of increasing literacy demands and increasing business sophistication, most students may need some training in business. Traditional teaching methods once used to teach smaller numbers of competent students are no longer adequate to do the job. When a subject is so popular, teachers cannot and should not teach only to the top 15 to 20 percent of the student population.

DEMANDS FOR FUNCTIONAL LITERACY

There is a steadily increasing demand for literacy in our society. At the time of the Revolutionary War, when blacksmiths, trappers, farmers, and craftspeople didn't need to read, experts estimate that only 15 percent of the population could read and write. By the time of the Civil War this figure had almost doubled to 28 percent. But literacy didn't really become a concern until the beginning of the twentieth century, when immigrants flooded into America.

During World War I the Army tested men for the draft and found that 25 percent were unable to read a newspaper or write a simple sentence. In 1941 all men who could not pass a test of fourth-grade reading ability were to be rejected as illiterate, according to an Army directive. In the World War II draft, 3.8 percent of white and 11.2 percent of black draftees were rejected.

According to census statistics, today's Americans are more literate than ever before. A 1969 study reported that 99 percent of the population over age 14 could read and write a simple message in English or another language. In 1970, 76 percent of 17-year-olds completed high school.(5)

We have steadily progressed toward total literacy. But the ability to read and write a simple message will no longer suffice. Higher levels of performance are necessary to cope with life in our developed society. Every day citizens are expected to fill out forms; read and understand installment contracts, insurance policies, warranties, and labels; decipher manuals; and keep abreast of what's happening in newspapers and magazines. One goal of secondary education is to help students improve the quality of their literacy so that they can adapt to the society that will confront them upon graduation.

NEED FOR RETRAINING

Elementary school students read for different purposes and in different ways than do older students and adults. Most of their written material is in narrative form. Concepts and new vocabulary are presented slowly, so students have a chance to comprehend them.

But when students enter middle school or junior high school, they are faced with a different type of reading task. Narration is replaced by exposition, which is more difficult to read. New vocabulary may be almost overwhelming. The limited experiences of students may not have prepared them for the new concepts introduced in their texts. Rather than reading to find out "what happens to the main character," students are asked to derive information—facts, names, dates, specific details—and interpret what they read for its bias or completeness. Texts, especially those in many business skills courses, may include detailed instructions to follow.

Teachers cannot assume that students have learned to read in elementary school. Though most students have learned to read to some degree, they have not received instruction on how to approach a difficult business text, how to interpret tables, or how to use the information they have just read.

Good readers engage in a complex type of mental activity characterized by a controlled sort of stream of consciousness. When these students read, their thoughts are directed and focused. They can put the ideas they read into an orderly pattern for future use. Reading is an interaction, a communication between author and reader. Reading must involve ideas, background, common language, common interest, and a mutual point of departure. Practical reading is nearly impossible until a basic foundation of shared background, language, and goals is established. It is the job of business teachers to promote that interaction. They need to know when texts are used as resource handbooks and when they are used as idea stimulators.

Teachers need to recognize student weaknesses and anticipate areas where students need to grow. New vocabulary and new concepts are two key areas where students generally need help from the teacher. A bookkeeping textbook may contain a dozen or more new words in a single chapter. Students may have no knowledge of a new term and may lack the background to see how the new word fits into the whole. Other words (such as *abstract, charge,* and *statement*) may have technical meanings that students do not know. Students also usually need some guidance in organization of ideas; easy use of terms and ideas; and special skills, such as using charts and graphs. These tasks apply to textbook as well as nontextbook materials.

In a very real sense, then, business teachers need to train their students to meet the demands of specialized business reading—to lead them from the identification of new and unfamiliar words to the manipulation of vocabulary and ideas in the business world.

SKILLS DEVELOPED IN BUSINESS COURSES

Students who perform well in one business class may do poorly in another. Though this is in part attributable to differences among teachers, the time of day the class is offered, or changes in a student's personal life, many such failures are the direct result of differing reading skills required in each course.

In general, business education courses can be classified into two categories: skills courses such as typewriting and shorthand, and nonskills concept courses such as business law or business economics. These two kinds of courses require very different kinds of reading. In some business classes, reading techniques learned in social studies, English, math, and science classes are appropriate. Textbooks for skills courses may have many directions to follow. In contrast, textbooks for concept courses contain mostly expository material, similar to those in a social studies class. Typewriting and shorthand, in particular, require word recognition skills. General business and bookkeeping require more in the way of comprehension skills, critical evaluation, and ability to locate materials and information quickly

and accurately. Students in transcription and office practice classes frequently need help in developing their oral reading ability. Learning a vocabulary of special symbols is essential in shorthand, typewriting, business arithmetic, and retailing but not in general business, consumer economics, or business law. The ability to draw conclusions from a textbook may be required in bookkeeping, retailing, or business law but usually not in typewriting and shorthand.

One large high school listed all courses offered in the business department and the reading skills pertinent to each course. (See Appendix A, Text Reference I.)(4) Business teachers don't have to teach all these skills from scratch, but they should anticipate having to fill in gaps for many students.

SUMMARY

One goal of business teachers is to develop independent, competent students who seek out and enjoy learning about new professional and personal interests. This goal is especially important for today's students who must be versatile enough to retrain for changing occupational demands. The ability to learn independently using printed materials is a lifetime competency that business education students need to develop.

Reading a business textbook differs from reading poetry, short stories, or novels. Specialized reading skills and abilities are needed to master business reading, and these skills are rarely learned in traditional English classes. Business teachers are the professionals most competent at teaching "business literacy," since they have clearer ideas on what is important in using business texts.

The brighter and more competent students have always been capable of learning new skills with a minimum of direct teaching. The student population in business classes has expanded, however, to include larger numbers of average and below average students. This new group can benefit from the direct teaching of business reading skills. A successful business curriculum will have to incorporate both textbook readings and readings from the "real world" of business. Any other approach is likely to lead to a good deal of frustration and failure for both students and teachers.

2. ASSESSMENT TECHNIQUES

Business education teachers are being forced to reassess their teaching techniques in light of increased enrollments and a wider range of student ability within the classroom. Business education teachers can no longer assume that all students have mastered the prerequisite skills necessary for success with business education assignments.

Frustrated teachers acknowledge this lack of prerequisite skills when they complain, "The kids simply can't read what's required. Send them back to elementary school." The answer, however, is not so simple. Business reading calls upon generalized reading ability, to be sure, but it also requires a specialized way of viewing material and a specialized set of skills that have very little to do with the kind of reading techniques taught in elementary school or in a remedial reading class. Some students with perfectly acceptable reading test scores experience some reading difficulty in some business education courses.

Reading specialized business material is a fairly complicated process, and it is a process that elementary teachers and English teachers cannot really teach. Business education teachers are the professionals most competent to analyze and teach these techniques. A teacher cannot simply say to students, "Read these pages," because students may attempt to read the assignment as if it were a story or perhaps part of a history text. The teacher needs to analyze the assignment in order to help students find the best reading approach. No doubt, certain parts of the assignment are more important than other parts. Perhaps students need to be reminded to glance back and forth between graphs and copy. Help students determine beforehand which terms and concepts are important enough to be noted and learned. Explain that the strategies and processes used to read descriptions differ from those used to read directions. Some passages need to be taken quite literally, others require interpretation and some degree of background knowledge. If the textbook is wordy, remind students to skim the wordy material until they come across a new idea that warrants a slower pace.

Gaps in a student's ability to read business education materials can often be dealt with quite briefly by the classroom teacher. When making an assignment, take an extra five minutes to "talk through" a chapter, demonstrating how to handle rough passages. If only a few students are experiencing a certain reading problem, they can be given the special instruction in a group while the rest of the class works ahead on the assignment.

PREREQUISITE SKILLS

All of this presumes, of course, that business education teachers know which reading skills are prerequisites for success and can assess which students lack these skills. The list of prerequisite skills differs, of course, from one business education class to another and from one teacher to another. There are, however, certain general questions that a teacher can use to assess student abilities:

1. Which students are able to read and understand typical passages?

2. Which students are able to concentrate on a reading task for 15 minutes or more?

3. Which students can accurately retrieve information from graphs and tables?

4. Which students already have mastered the basic concepts necessary for understanding new ideas presented in the course?

5. Which students read text material quickly enough to complete assignments in a reasonable amount of time?

6. Which students can uncover the author's structure or pattern of thought?

7. Which students can apply what they read to other knowledge they have gained?

8. Which students can identify main ideas and sort them out from isolated details?

9. Which students can use the index and table of contents to find information?

10. Which students can use context clues to define new words?

11. Which students can quickly assimilate new vocabulary and concepts?

12. Which students can follow directions?

Of course, the teacher of a particular class may wish to add a few specialized abilities to this list. For example, the special symbol-to-concept relationship learned in a shorthand class requires particular abilities, as does the critical reading required in an advanced business law course.

INFORMAL STUDENT ASSESSMENT AND RECORDKEEPING

Rather than discover at midsemester grading that "half the students can't read," an aware business teacher can avoid wasted efforts by acting on early knowledge of which students can read which kinds of material. For example, if six students can't use charts effectively, it is pointless to ask those students to read a chapter filled with charts until they have received 5 to 10 minutes of instruction in that skill. Other students in the class can be given some reading time while the teacher works with this small group. If a more sizable number of students are unable to read charts, the in-class instruction time can be expanded. Teachers who proceed cautiously at the beginning of the semester increase the likelihood that most of the class will be able to keep up with assignments by the middle and end of the semester. Most seasoned business teachers have suffered the uncomfortable experience of facing blank stares from large numbers of students who couldn't keep up. The wise business teacher can avoid this experience by being aware of potential roadblocks and spending a few extra minutes in class teaching those students who are stalled because they lack an easily learned skill.

During the first two or three weeks of class, create brief (5 to 10 minute) assignments to measure student abilities. For example, on the first day students can be asked to read three or four typical passages from the text and answer a few questions to test their grasp of main ideas. As the class is reading, the teacher can note which students are unable to attend to this assignment for even a 15-minute block of time. Five-minute exercises during other class periods can help a teacher determine which students are able to use graphs and charts, which read rapidly enough to complete homework in a reasonable amount of time, and which can use text guides like the index and table of contents. A short quiz can assess premastery of basic concepts, and early application assignments can single out those students experiencing difficulty with the more sophisticated business reading skills outlined in points six through eight.

Most of this information would normally surface some time during the course of a semester. The business teacher who wants to make an informal diagnosis of possible problem areas simply makes sure students experience a full sampling of reading tasks during the first two weeks.

Recordkeeping can be limited to a single sheet of paper attached to the teacher's grade book. Students can be listed down a lefthand column, and general business reading skills (such as text comprehension, 15-minute concentration, graphs and tables, and basic concepts) can be listed across the top of the sheet. (See Appendix A, Text Reference II.) A student who demonstrates competence with graphs receives a (+). Other students may receive a (√) or a (−) depending on their abilities. These lower marks should be made in pencil so they can be changed when a skill is mastered.

Before making reading assignments, the teacher should determine which abilities are required to complete that assignment successfully. A particular assignment may call for the heavy use of two or three prerequisite skills listed above. The teacher can glance down the appropriate columns to determine if the majority of students have mastered these skills. If all three columns are dominated by (+) marks, the teacher can proceed with confidence. If there is a sprinkling of (√) and (−) marks, these few students will need a little special attention. If the columns show only a few (+) marks, the teacher should postpone the assignment until most of the class has mastered the prerequisite skills.

ASSESSMENT OF TEXTBOOKS AND READING MATERIALS

The books and materials that students read in

business classes have distinguishing characteristics. Here are some considerations to keep in mind when evaluating textbooks, pamphlets, and other materials:

1. *Interest: variety and intensity*—Will the material be of interest to students? Does it appeal to a variety of interests?

2. *Inference requirements*—Is the writing style straightforward or does it require a high degree of deduction and inference?

3. *Vocabulary and concept load*—Is the vocabulary difficult or technical or both? Are new concepts presented so quickly that students cannot assimilate them successfully?

4. *Organizational aids*—Does the format use numerous subheads or other means to help the reader organize thoughts and guide the movement of ideas?

5. *Relevant examples*—Does the author use current examples from the world of business to illustrate points? Are the examples illustrated and explained in the text? The more unfamiliar the concept, the more examples are needed.

6. *Readability level*—Is the material too difficult or too easy for most students? Is it sensibly close to most students' ability or shockingly distant?

7. *Student appeal*—Is the material displayed attractively, or does it turn students off? Are the pictures too juvenile? Does the material look "adult"?

8. *Professionalism*—Do supplemental materials gathered or designed by the teacher show careful attention to details such as proper punctuation and crisp press? Are materials similar to those which students will encounter in the business world?

If class reading materials do not measure up against this set of criteria, the business teacher will have to work harder to bridge the gaps between the students and the text. If the gaps are wide in the areas of interest, vocabulary, and relevant examples, the teacher will need to bridge those gaps *before* students do the reading—perhaps by preteaching vocabulary and discussing the specific concepts mentioned in the text. In addition, the teacher should take care to present the material in a way that accents its relevance and motivates students to actually read the text. If readability and inference requirements are overly high, the teacher will find it necessary to break chapters down into smaller chunks and simplify assignments.

The metaphor of the business teacher as bridge drives home a painful point. If the text is quite distant from student abilities, the teacher can expect to be in constant service as a bridge. The traffic will be heavy, and wear and tear on the structure will soon be evident. Teachers who find themselves having to constantly bridge gaps between students and reading materials are wise to seek supplemental materials and texts that don't require so much bridging.

ASSESSMENT METHODS

Once business education teachers have a clear idea of what is required for reading success in their classes, they can begin to determine which students meet the requirements, which need a little help, and which need a great deal of help. It is important that the business education teacher assess the specific strengths and weaknesses of students early in the semester to avoid teaching above or below their abilities.

There are several ways to accomplish this assessment. These include (1) careful observation of student behavior, (2) informal exercises in textbook use, (3) teacher-constructed reading tests, and (4) the practice of giving pre-unit quizzes or exercises to spot those students who can work independently and those who need teacher help in order to succeed.

Teacher Observation

Although it is extremely difficult for secondary school teachers to make detailed observations about every student early in the semester, certain students quickly distinguish themselves on the basis of either their outstanding ability or their problems. Bamman, Hogan, and Greene(1) suggest that several characteristics observable in the classroom can help business education teachers identify students with reading problems:

- the student who never finishes an assignment

- the student who complains that assignments are too long

- the student who frequently makes excuses for lack of progress

- the student who exhibits poor work habits

- the student who habitually withdraws from reading

- the student who is apparently capable of responding to oral instruction or discussion but is frustrated when confronted by a reading assignment

- the student who makes mistakes because he or she does not read directions carefully

- the student who tries to answer a bookkeeping or accounting question without looking at the detailed information provided

- the student who recognizes few complex or multisyllable words in typewriting class

- the student who has problems transcribing shorthand into coherent prose.

Students who exhibit a number of these behaviors may also fail to meet the reading prerequisites of the business class (see the checklist on page 15). It is important that business education teachers identify such students as early in the semester as possible. Early detection allows several options for both student and teacher. If the student is having only a few difficulties, short-term early help can avoid long-term failure. If reading difficulties are widespread, a reading specialist can be consulted. In the meantime the student can participate in special grouping and tutoring sessions early in the year to improve chances for success later in the year.

Business teachers must be especially alert and observant to detect the barely literate "nice kids" who remain quiet in class, behave with social courtesy and even leadership, and give a clear impression of trying to do assignments. These students have the potential for doing well, but often fail to elicit the early attention of classroom teachers who are more aware of the disruptive brand of disabled reader. Organized observation of student reading behaviors can help teachers identify such students in time to help them.

Informal Exercises in Textbook Use

Since it is often difficult to settle down to content instruction during the first few class sessions, some teachers have found this to be a good time to administer a quiz or inventory on textbook reading skills. In doing this, the teacher is not taking time away from instruction, but rather learning which areas need more or less emphasis. In addition, this assessment can tell the teacher what kinds of problems students might encounter with the text, so the teacher is able to attack them early in the semester, before students become frustrated or overwhelmed with the work.

The best way to discover how students read the text and other assigned materials is to use those materials in designing a test or inventory of reading skills. Such an inventory can be tailored for the specific business class—typewriting, bookkeeping, business law, and so on. The test assesses student competence in skills such as understanding word meanings through context, noting main ideas, gaining information from pictures or graphs, and using parts of the text (the glossary, index, or tables).

There are several advantages to developing a teacher-made inventory of the text and other reading materials. The inventory or pretest can be scheduled at the teacher's convenience unlike standardized reading tests that are often scheduled at the convenience of administrators. By basing the inventory on materials the student will use, the pretest is both more pertinent and more related to class objectives. If the pretest is scheduled early in the semester, it provides immediate diagnostic information. Because it is geared to the course material, questions can be similar to those in assignments. Also, this kind of test or inventory is easy to score because it is not "graded"; rather it is used to pinpoint the strengths and needs of individual students. In fact, students can benefit from correcting the inventories in class, with discussion about the accuracy and appropriateness of specific responses. In this sense, the inventory becomes a teaching tool. Having the students correct their own papers can objectify their self-assessment of strengths and needs. Students are much more open to accept help in a nongraded situation such as this one. The teacher can administer similar tests throughout the school year to determine student progress. For a sample of textbook inventory items, see Appendix A, Test Reference III.

Teacher-Constructed Reading Tests

Some teachers have found they cannot rely on standardized test scores to predict student ability to read business materials. Rather than test the reading ability of students and then compute the reading difficulty of the textbook, some teachers combine the two processes by using a simple technique called the cloze procedure. The cloze procedure gives the teacher a means to test comprehension of a passage and determine whether the text is written at the student's reading level. By eliminating every fifth _____ in a text and _____ the student try to _____ in the exact word _____ that the author used, _____ teacher can get a _____ accurate idea of how _____ the student comprehended the _____.

The term "cloze" is taken from the psychological concept of closure. Closure refers to the human tendency to fill in or complete an entity that appears to be incomplete. For example, when you see a broken circle, your tendency is to draw a line in the blank space. The same thing happens with language. When a speaker is searching for a word to finish a sentence, someone will often come up with a word to fill the gap. The ability to supply the correct word reflects a good deal of background with the topic being discussed, a well developed and internalized sense of syntax, and a sense of the tone of previous sentences. A student able to correctly

supply a reasonable percentage of missing words is using the skills that a good reader must use.

To construct a cloze test, take a selection of at least 275 words that is not dependent on immediately preceding information. Beginning with the second sentence, delete every fifth word, using blanks of one length for all deleted words. Ideally the passage will contain 50 blanks. The students then read the passage and fill in the blanks, usually in about 20 minutes. Only those words that *exactly* match the words of the original are counted. This strict counting procedure enables teachers to use the scoring criteria developed by researchers in this field.(2) Students able to identify at least 41 percent of the words deleted are considered able to comprehend the text. Scores below 41 percent indicate inadequate comprehension. Bormuth found the following equivalencies between successful cloze responses and answers on a typical multiple choice comprehension test:

Percent of cloze blanks correct	Percent of comprehension items passed
50	95
40	80
35	65

In order to fill in the blanks, the student must read actively, paying attention to context clues that are crucial to deciding on the missing word. Because the cloze test requires that the student think along in the language of the author and make heavy use of context, the teacher can make educated guesses about the student's familiarity with the vocabulary and his or her ability with context. However, rather than develop hard-and-fast criteria from a cloze test, it makes more sense to use the results as a way to identify individuals who need closer observation.

Teachers who use the cloze procedure should remember that 50 percent is the highest score that should be expected. If a student has missed 70 to 80 percent of the items and if replaced words make no sense in the context of passage, the student needs special attention from the business teacher and perhaps from a reading specialist. Failure in the cloze procedure suggests the student will find reading the text a frustrating, failure-prone experience. However, some newspaper and magazine articles or perhaps pamphlets and free government publications may be within the student's ability range.

Business teachers can assess the true limits of a student's reading ability by having on hand several such articles and pamphlets, ranging from those that are quite simple to those that are nearly as difficult as the textbook. For each sample of material, the teacher can develop three to five comprehension questions. These questions should be typed on an index card attached to the reading. Students can read the passages silently or orally and then answer the questions for the teacher out loud. Silent reading avoids embarrassment and some social pressure, but oral reading has the advantage of alerting the teacher to specific word and vocabulary difficulties. It is up to the teacher to determine the most appropriate method for each student.

The student should be asked to read the most simple material first so that a backlog of reading success and confidence is developed. The reading should progress through increasingly difficult passages until the student begins to evidence difficulty with comprehension. Students who miss more than half the comprehension questions or misread or mispronounce between 5 and 10 percent of the words read orally are experiencing reading frustration. For such students, a certain proportion of reading assignments will have to be at an easier level if they are to have a chance of improving to the level of the class textbook.

A good deal more diagnosis can be done to determine the origin and nature of student reading disabilities. However, unless the business teacher has received special training in this area, it is wise to seek the help of a reading specialist. Given the time limitations experienced by most classroom teachers, it is unreasonable to expect the business teacher to do much more than identify a student's reading level accurately enough to match that student with business reading materials of appropriate difficulty.

STUDY HABITS ASSESSMENT

Some students who experience reading diffi-

culty with textbook assignments may score reasonably well on textbook inventories and cloze tests. In these cases it is wise to take the student aside and ask why the student is experiencing difficulty. If no clear answer emerges, it may be that the student has poor study habits and is ignorant of his or her deficiency in this area. Most adolescents find it extremely difficult to sit quietly alone with a book and a sheet of paper and concentrate. Those who have a setting and a system for study are more likely to persist in studying. The setting can reduce the influence of competing attractions in the environment. Having a study system gets students through an assignment efficiently so that time remains for other attractions. If students can devise their own rituals for study, they are much more likely to make studying a regular and important part of their lives.

Business teachers can help students develop their awareness of personal study habits by having them complete a checklist at the beginning of each new grading period. This checklist (see Appendix A, Text Reference IV) can help students reach their own conclusions about where improvements are needed in the weeks to come.

Teachers can help students organize for study by giving assignments and scheduling test dates well in advance, perhaps even making up a monthly "calendar of events" for the classroom. Some teachers use planned study sessions to apply specific study techniques, and this can help students devise their own study routines. Teachers can also show students how to work in pairs or small groups, using questions and answers to reinforce the learning of new material. Have students formulate their own questions, but be sure that each student is both a question-asker and an answer-giver.

SUMMARY

This chapter has examined several formal and informal techniques the business education teacher can use to assess student reading readiness. These techniques include:

1. informal assessment of the prerequisites for reading success

2. teacher observation of student reading behaviors

3. the use of textbook inventories

4. teacher-constructed reading tests such as the cloze procedure and brief graduated readings.

Students who score high in these assessments may still experience difficulties arising from poor study settings and study habits.

The business education teacher can maximize chances for student success by making such assessments early in the school year. With this information, prerequisites can be taught and students can be matched with business reading materials of appropriate difficulty.

3. ORGANIZING THE BUSINESS CLASSROOM AND STUDENTS FOR INSTRUCTION

Each person allots time in different ways. Some use time efficiently, while others fritter away enormous amounts of time. Teachers encounter time limits as grim realities reinforced by bells and deadlines. The constant round of routine tasks required by the school administration or by the department can be immensely frustrating. Teachers want to get to know their students so they can help them progress as far as possible. But there just isn't enough time to get to know every student on an individual basis.

Or is there? No one teacher can be expected to singlehandedly tutor on an individual basis nearly 150 students with varying levels of reading ability, interest in business subjects, and motivation. Once teachers accept this limitation, they have made the first step toward organizing the classroom for instruction. To organize, a teacher must:

1. draw upon student resources for help

2. plan lessons with a maximum of student learning activity and a minimum of teacher-centered activity

3. organize the time and space of the classroom so students will know what is supposed to be happening and where things are.

THE TEACHER AS EXECUTIVE

Think back a moment to the one-room schoolhouse. The single all-grades teacher did not expect to meet the needs of each student minute-by-minute during the school day, because it was obvious that one person couldn't do it all. So students taught other students—of necessity. Materials and tasks had to be clearly organized and available, and individual students were responsible for certain tasks on a daily basis. As a result, the well-organized teacher had large portions of time to devote to individual students. The teacher was, in a sense, the executive of a learning organization.

Today's teachers can emulate the one-room schoolhouse executive. Rather than try to do every-thing and always be the center of attention, the business teacher can look carefully at what really needs to be done. The teacher can then ask for help from the students. Any teacher who can be replaced by a high school student probably ought to be. Surprised? Consider some of the simple tasks teachers do, the large amounts of wasted time. Freeing oneself of some of these tasks allows teachers to have increased time for individual students. This approach also leads students to be more involved in their own learning by helping others learn.

Any business executive who refused to delegate authority and responsibility for performing simple tasks would not survive for long. Any business education classroom that revolves around teacher efforts cannot hope to accomplish much in terms of educational goals *or* individual student development. Like any executive, the business educator needs to organize activity, students, resources, and available time.

ORGANIZING ACTIVITY

One of the first things to do is develop a classroom atmosphere of cooperative learning. In a cooperative relationship, more than one leader emerges. The teacher is not the only person who can answer questions or deal with problems.

The wise teacher creates incentives that encourage students to become leaders. If a teacher takes on the additional job of assistant track coach, he or she receives extra pay for increased responsibilities. If the team does well in meets, the coach is showered with appreciation from students, parents, and athletes. Some persons may even agree to help coach the team because they like the prestige of coaching or because they like the physical activity. Some or all of these factors might motivate the coach to keep working. Classroom teachers can similarly draw upon such motivators as social prestige and appreciation to foster student leadership.

Some teachers might use a point system and allot extra points to students who take on necessary tasks. Depending on classroom needs, these tasks could include:

- taking attendance
- recording daily work
- getting out materials and making sure they are returned
- keeping track of the week's assignments for one's group or row (very helpful in catching up for absent students)
- tutoring a classmate on a particular assignment
- putting up bulletin boards and making displays
- gathering supplementary materials for coming units
- tallying lunchroom lists, etc., as required by the administration.

There are really no limits to this list. Many of the teacher's daily tasks can be done at least partially by responsible, trained adolescents. Of course students must see the jobs as worth having. Jobs should be rotated from time to time—especially if students are not performing them well.

Providing such tasks serves several constructive purposes. The teacher will be freed to reach more students. Students will have the opportunity to organize their thinking, apply reading and writing skills, and receive positive reinforcement for using skills they've just learned. Teachers should not feel guilty about "using" students, unless their motive is simply to avoid doing any work. The measure of one's worth as a teacher is not how much of the necessary busywork a teacher can singlehandedly complete, but rather how much students learn.

ORGANIZING STUDENTS

The business classroom is the natural place for students to learn the habit of taking responsibility for what is going on around them. Very few employers tolerate employees who must constantly be told *exactly* what to do and then have the instructions repeated ten minutes later. This pattern is common, however, in business classrooms. Administrators and executives do not allow themselves to become mired in petty details and requests the way many business teachers do. Executives delegate authority, expect cooperation, and provide incentives for regular responsible activity. In contrast, in many classrooms incentives encourage students to do as little as possible to scrape by. Business teachers need to apply what they know about business management to the organization and operation of their own classes.

ORGANIZING TIME

Business teachers who cannot find the time to work individually with students need to do a time study of their job. What tasks currently demand time? What tasks could be accomplished if more time were available? These two lists of tasks can be examined for possible delegation.

The goal is not only to release the teacher to handle individual reading difficulties, but also to develop responsible, independent adolescent learners. The awarding of points, teacher praise, and the pleasure of responsibility can serve as incentives that encourage students to take on teacher-identified jobs. Students who perform well can be promoted to even more responsible positions, and students who don't perform well can be temporarily "fired." Successful completion of class assignments over a specified time period will again qualify a "fired" student for "hiring consideration."

One way to encourage and teach student independence is to post assignments or directions in a particular place. A student might be "hired" to record assignments and then be responsible for posting them. Tardy students or returning absentees can be directed by row leaders to the posted assignments. Few young persons can listen carefully enough to retain a complicated set of directions. By listing daily directions and expectations on the board, the teacher can quickly check the progress of individuals or groups. "Who has completed part three?" the teacher can ask, and see immediately which students need some help and which are ready for other activities.

Nearly every class has two or three students

who complete assignments and must wait for others. The teacher as executive frees such students for more productive work as team leaders. Team leaders can choose "editors" to proofread material before it is submitted to the teacher for inspection. Other team leaders can monitor the progress of material as typewriting classes work to produce final copy. Still other teams can monitor the duplication and the binding of rewritten chapters so that next semester's poorer readers can use these in lieu of overly difficult textbooks.

Similar work projects can be organized to handle the tutoring of less able students. Tutoring can occur completely within the classroom, or capable seniors can be released to work with less capable sophomores. Again, responsible tutors are rewarded and irresponsible students are terminated and must rejoin the dull ranks of students who are only allowed to work on regular assignments.

Some student teams can gather supplementary business reading material by drafting letters to businesses or government offices. The whole process of compiling addresses, drafting letters, and typing acceptable copy, can create a wealth of jobs that teach business skills while reinforcing reading and writing skills.

Such work should not be scheduled every day but can be fitted into the class schedule one or two days a week. Business teachers who use such methods have been pleased to find that students are able to do five day's worth of work in four days if student efforts are rewarded with more responsible activity.

These kinds of work projects are fun, meaningful, and useful. It is not often one can say so much about a classroom activity. If the prerequisite for admission to such meaningful work is the successful completion of class assignments, many students will be motivated to succeed.

Business teachers who orchestrate activity in this way can be freed to direct valuable attention to individual students most in need of professional help. A special group of three or four students can have direct access to the teacher for up to 20 minutes. The teacher now has time to question and encourage two or three sophomores being tutored by seniors. A few minutes of class time can even be used to examine the suitability of supplementary reading material gathered by a student work group.

Stranding Assignments

Business education courses are usually divided into blocks of 50 to 60 minutes. This traditional arrangement, based on the university system, can create problems for business teachers attempting to use reading in their secondary school classes.

In the university each class or lecture develops a new topic or a new aspect of a larger topic. Concepts are introduced chronologically or logically and are presented one at a time, each block building upon the previous block. Lectures are given twice a week, and professors assume that students will assimilate concepts and reinforce lecture ideas with assigned or extra readings. By and large this system works for the motivated, capable learners one finds in a university where students pay for the opportunity to learn.

Teachers must deal with a different population in most high school business classes. In addition to maturity and motivational differences, many secondary students have short attention spans, usually 15 to 20 minutes. Consequently, the one topic per day pattern is not very likely to succeed in the high school classroom.

An alternative plan is *stranding*, a relatively simple technique for organizing time and reading/learning goals. Rather than planning one learning goal and activity for Monday, another for Tuesday, a third for Wednesday, and so forth, a teacher lists the goals for the week and then strands them to spread them across five days. This is the concept underlying the popular "Sesame Street," where several different topics are treated during each program.

A few examples will clarify this concept. A Distributive Education class, in which students learn partially through reading, might have some of the following reading goals:

1. increased technical vocabulary

2. mastery of major textbook concepts about advertising

3. ability to read and follow product warranties and guarantees

4. ability to observe, apply, and express textbook concepts in new situations

5. increased interest in and reading of business-related materials.

In a traditional time organization, the teacher might spend a class period or perhaps two teaching each goal. A day might be spent on vocabulary, a day or two spent lecturing or discussing the text, a day spent working with actual products, and a major end-of-unit test, with perhaps some mention of extra credit reading available in the library.

In a traditional time organization each day builds completely upon the preceding day. If students are absent or inattentive, they miss material and find it difficult to make up what they have missed. Most information must be learned in one exposure, despite the established principle of learning theory that distributed learning is much more effective. Furthermore, the Distributive Education class is but one of six classes during a student's day. Each teacher makes the same implicit demand: "Get it today because tomorrow we'll be covering another concept."

Stranding, on the other hand, considers academic goals in terms of several short activities that can be spread across the week. During any given day, the reading/learning activity changes several times as each goal is touched upon. The changes in activity keep attention high and the repeated reinforcement increases the likelihood that students will master the material, even if they miss a class due to illness.

In order to strand, a teacher must resist the temptation to plan one day at a time and begin to consider week-long or unit-long priorities and goals. The reading goals and activities for the Distributive Education class mentioned earlier might look something like this:

- Increased business vocabulary

  a. five-minute exercise using special root words—for example: consumption, promotional, or expenditure

  b. textbook scavenger hunt to find key unit words in context

  c. student spotting of unknown words during brief chapter previews

- Mastery of textbook concepts about advertising

  a. 10-15 minute chapter preview for main ideas (perhaps including brief outlining)

  b. condensing a portion of the chapter to one or two pages

  c. reading summary passages written by other students

  d. using text to answer student supplied questions

- Ability to read and follow product warranties or guarantees

  a. outlining major points of document

  b. explaining to another student what is and is not covered

  c. being corrected by another student for missed points

- Ability to observe, apply, and express textbook concepts in other situations

  a. identifying advertising approaches in the media

  b. creating and writing comprehension questions based on the chapter

  c. trading questions with other students and answering questions in discussion groups

  d. estimating advertising costs in print media

- Increased interest in and reading of business-related materials

  a. scavenger hunt for related articles in magazines and newspapers (homework)

  b. extra credit project for top students listing books, pamphlets, and articles available in library

  c. letter-writing project—students request materials from appropriate businesses and advertising agencies

d. reading of appropriate business-oriented novels

e. locating, reading, and summarizing on index cards interesting portions of other texts found in the classroom or library

f. creating a project of one's own.

Once the teacher has selected a few main goals and a variety of alternative reading activities for achieving those goals, time can be stranded. The example shown in Appendix A, Text Reference V is based on a five-day, 50-60 minute schedule, although the same principle can be applied to any time framework. This same sort of stranded structure can be used for almost any business class. Since a major characteristic of stranding is having several activities emphasize a few basic goals, the structure is flexible. If an activity doesn't seem productive, it can be dropped or exchanged for a different activity from the next day. If an activity goes particularly well, it can be extended at the expense of another activity. Since each major objective is approached from many different directions, it is no longer necessary for each individual activity to be the final experience *par excellence.*

APPLICATION OF PRINCIPLES TO SPECIFIC BUSINESS EDUCATION CLASSES

General Techniques for Business Courses

Stranding is only one technique that business education teachers can use to improve student reading abilities. There are several other easy-to-accomplish activities available, including the following:

1. Determine academic readiness for reading the assigned materials. If students are ready for a task, it becomes fulfilling to perform that task. Students who are not prepared will be frustrated and will develop poor attitudes that make later teaching more difficult.

2. Check the reading difficulty of assigned textbooks and supplementary reading materials. Some materials are too difficult; others are too juvenile. The teacher must look for a match between material and learners.

3. Show students how to preview reading material for main ideas. Students become more self-reliant and need less teacher direction.

4. Show students how to vary their style of reading to fit the material and purpose. Variation in reading speed is widely used in business. For example, business correspondence should be skimmed to see from where it comes and what kind of attention it requires. Skimming gives the reader a chance to decide if he or she is to handle the letter (in which case it may require more careful reading) or if it should be routed elsewhere.

5. Help students locate supplementary reading material on the subject. For example, in an office practice class, students need to learn how to locate materials quickly and find useful references. Students also need to be familiar with government publications, know why they were written, and be able to relate information to experience.

6. Help students improve their specialized vocabulary. Some teachers use index cards with words on one side and meanings on the other. Another approach is structural analysis, in which students break down words to learn the meaning of prefixes, suffixes, and common roots.

In addition to these six techniques, teachers can also help students proofread, read in thought units, interpret graphs and charts, use dictionaries properly, develop comprehension, and understand textbook content.

If textbooks are grossly inappropriate for students, teachers should be willing to write letters of criticism to publishers and authors. One author who received several hundred comments from teachers on a textbook tried to incorporate their wishes into revisions, new editions, and new textbooks.

If a text or part of a text is extremely inappropriate for some students, don't struggle along with it. Enlist the cooperation of some of the better students and the school librarian to compile bibliographies of related materials. Outside reading such as this helps establish the relevance of the course to today's world. Such projects also provide important responsibility-building tasks for students— while freeing the teacher to do a better job.

Because classes in the business curriculum differ widely, the reading skills necessary for success also differ. The courses can, however, be broken into two groups: skill courses and nonskill courses. Skill courses such as typewriting, shorthand, and bookkeeping presume that students can follow directions and use so-called "how-to-do-it" textbooks. Nonskill courses such as business law, general business, business economics, and marketing require different sorts of reading techniques.

Skill Courses: Reading Directions

Business teachers typically complain that students just can't follow written directions. Because directions comprise a large portion of the textbooks and tasks in typewriting, shorthand, and other business skills classes, it is essential that teachers help students learn to read directions better.

Improvement in the reading of directions is an investment that can pay off in considerable time saved, as students eliminate nonessential questions, require less supervision, and work through practice after practice more accurately and quickly. To upgrade the reading of directions, business teachers can use a variety of techniques. A good lead-in activity that emphasizes the need and purpose of having directions is to give students a page of copy without directions. Later the teacher can point out direction-giving clues in the text by asking students, "How do the authors focus your attention on exactly what you are to do? By the type and size of print? Use of color? Other means?" By recognizing which blocks of type are directions, students can be alerted to use their "direction-reading" style when necessary.

Another technique is to help the class develop a checklist to evaluate themselves. The following kinds of questions are helpful: "Do you make sure you understand the meaning of unfamiliar key terms?" and "Do you examine photographs and drawings?"

Taking class time to practice and model reading directions can also be useful. Some teachers ask students to use a three-step approach before beginning assignments: (1) skim the directions; (2) underline all key words, which are usually nouns and verbs; and (3) paraphrase the directions, perhaps by explaining them to a classmate who listens carefully to hear if anything was left out or misunderstood.

Another technique is to build from relatively simple to complex directions. Initially, students might be asked to follow one-step directions. As the week goes on, the teacher can provide two-step, three-step, and progressively more complicated directions.

Bookkeeping and Accounting

Textbooks in bookkeeping and accounting may be the most difficult for students. The writing style is concise and terse, similar to that found in math and physical science textbooks. A heavy vocabulary and concept load requires slow, meticulous reading for details. Technical examples may be common, but there are few anecdotes that bring reality to the examples. In addition, to succeed with the material, the student must understand the organization of each chapter and each section so that what is read can be used immediately. Directions must be read with precision so that information can be used to solve realistic problems.

The technical vocabulary in beginning bookkeeping is extremely heavy, especially in the early parts of the course. A study by F. Wayne House(1) found that one bookkeeping textbook introduced 33 technical terms in the first chapter alone. Most high school bookkeeping texts contain more than 200 technical terms. House also found that about 30 percent of the questions on tests covering the early parts of bookkeeping courses were designed to test student knowledge of technical terms.

It makes sense then to begin reading aid in

the area of technical vocabulary. Terms such as *assessed value, cashiers check, unearned premium,* and *round lot* will be completely unfamiliar to many students. In addition to these new words, students may also be confused by "old" words that take on new meanings in the context of bookkeeping. A football player knows one meaning of the word *charge* that is not applicable in the business classroom. A reader of condensed books knows one meaning of *abstract* that differs from its meaning in the context of *abstract of accounts receivable.* Other common words with special meanings are: *account, capital, claim, cost, credit, cycle, depreciate, extend, footing, interest, liability, paycheck, post, prove, register, ruling, savings, statement,* and *terms.* Each day a few of these words should be introduced on the board, written into sentences that provide a meaningful context. Some students may want to copy these sentences on posters for extra credit.

Teachers also need to be aware of which common words students can recognize and define in a general way but not precisely enough for the subject. Confusion over these words may cause the student, especially the less capable reader, to miss the precise meaning of the written material. For instance, words such as *data, concrete, expire,* and *quarter* may be misinterpreted. The key here is for the business teacher to anticipate and deal with problems before making a reading assignment.

Another vocabulary problem is that some bookkeeping terms are used interchangeably. Although the terms may have slightly different meanings, teachers tend to use them interchangeably in class discussion. A few such terms include:(2)

- analysis paper, work-sheet paper, working paper
- bad debt, bad account, uncollectable account
- cash on hand, cash balance, balance on hand
- proprietorship, net worth, capital
- minus asset, valuation account, reserve account
- principal of note, face of note

- profit and loss statement, operating statement, income statement, income and expense statement
- liabilities, debts, obligations.

Students should know the precise meanings of the different terms and be able to understand when they are interchanged. However, it minimizes confusion if at the beginning of the course or when the terms are first introduced, teachers use one term consistently. Students can learn and retain new vocabulary better if the teacher introduces a small number of words each day, rather than overwhelm students with a list of 25 words every Monday.

Teachers who want students to quickly assimilate the meaning of new words must try to associate the terms in some way with the students' everyday experiences. For example, a bicycle might be labelled an *asset.* The word *depreciation* takes on relevance when students consider it in terms of a car purchase. Relating student experiences to vocabulary can be an interesting challenge for both the student and teacher. Students can help create their own examples, perhaps working in small groups.

In interviewing bookkeeping students, House(3) found that nearly half reported they did not finish textbook reading assignments because they could not understand what they are reading. In fact, his study suggested that only 40 percent of the students were able to read the texts. This study was conducted in the early 1950s, a period when the bottom portion of today's students would have been dropouts. Perhaps even more of today's students would cite difficulties.

Reading difficulty is generally estimated by measuring average sentence length and word length. The longer the sentence and the longer the average word, the more difficult the reading. A study of two bookkeeping texts, using Flesch's "Reading Ease Chart," found the texts to parallel the reading levels of magazines such as *Harper's, New Yorker,* and *Business Week*—in other words, beyond the reading ability of more than 50 percent of the high school students.(2)

To make difficult texts accessible to a larger percentage of students, the teacher should make a special effort early in the semester to demonstrate how the textbook is organized, what it contains, and the many ways it can be used effectively. Students should learn and practice special textbook study techniques. The inventory of textbook reading skills discussed in Chapter 2 provides a useful starting point for a few brief lessons. The teacher can demonstrate how to use the illustrations, summary questions, charts, and study guides provided in the text. These skills may be taught early in the course or stranded throughout the first several weeks.

Teachers may wish to use the preview technique with reading assignments, using the class period for instruction rather than for testing and recitation. A preview helps students focus their attention on key points in the text. Some teachers use the preview to introduce one or two of the new words that will be encountered in the assignment. With this approach, students can begin their assignment under the watchful eye of the teacher and potential problems may be uncovered and solved within the class period.

Typewriting

Reading for typewriting classes is not always reading in the ordinary sense of deriving meaning from printed symbols. In typewriting classes, the first purpose of reading is to reproduce characters on a typewriter. This reading task requires attention to detail rather than to meaning. For many students, typing is their first head-on collision with detail. In addition to reading the textbook, typewriting students have to read correspondence, forms, tabulations, and manuscripts. Clearly a variety of reading strategies is necessary for success here.

The typewriting textbook may be filled with detailed data that the student must understand and arrange logically. Little anecdotal writing is included. Much of the text explains procedures and forms. The large technical vocabulary can pose problems even though students may have previously encountered such words as: *set, release, slide, press back, shift, approximate, thirds, turn back, circular, continuous,* and *alternately.*

The textbook readings contain a heavy pro-portion of directions, and this is the critical skill that causes the most trouble for poor readers. Often the directions are read superficially, and students are then unable to accomplish an entire task. Teachers can suggest that students vary their rates of reading, since the rate for directions may be considerably slower than the rate for copy to be typed.

With some technical material, students must read and understand copy that they type, which may necessitate skimming before typing. The teacher can help by identifying difficult words and thus help students develop their vocabularies so they do not have to type words letter by letter. With vocabulary development, the teacher may wish to provide a refresher lesson on syllabication and on word roots. Some teachers suggest that students read slowly and carefully and try to observe letters in groups or patterns.

In advanced typewriting classes, students can be encouraged to develop an editorial orientation. When skimming material before typing, the student can be taught to look for organizational patterns, parallel writing structures, and consistent use of tense. The ability to identify errors *before* typing is the mark of an advanced typist.

Teachers who are tired of complaining about students who type without thinking have developed several ways to stimulate students to think. Force students to think about meaning as they type by omitting some words. For example: We wish _____ that we _____ placing your unpaid bills _____ the hands _____ our attorney for _____ collection. Or ask students to type a few paragraphs according to specific directions, and then retype the material in their own words. This gets them reading and thinking in thought units rather than letter-by-letter. Students must also learn how to adjust their reading speed when they read straight copy.

One typewriting teacher, faced with a large group of remedial students, devised a drill to develop word-level typing ability into phrase-level typing ability. Advanced students received extra credit for preparing a set of slides that used (1) individual words, (2) two-word groups, and (2) three-word groups. These slides were used several times a week for about ten minutes. The teacher showed the slide, which was read in unison aloud by the entire class. Then an individual would read it aloud, and then the teacher would dictate the word or words. The goal was to work toward longer meaningful units. Another teacher developed a similar method using slash marks to indicate meaningful phrases that should be read and typed as one unit.

To keep motivation high, many typewriting teachers varied assignments. Students might receive extra credit for finding newspaper articles to copy. Classified ads from the newspaper give students practice in centering each line. Students who finish work early can be allowed to work on personal projects, creative writing, or other school subjects—so long as they use the typewriter. In some schools, the English, social studies, and science textbooks are rewritten for lower levels and students use typed copies of the rewritten materials.

Shorthand

Because shorthand is a code, the student is faced with a reading situation similar to the one encountered in mathematics and some science classes. In math and science, symbols, formulas, and equations can represent words or phrases. In much the same way, shorthand is a new form of written language.

The successful shorthand student must be able to hear sounds correctly and have a good grasp of the alphabetic symbols. Basic comprehension skills enable the student to organize information. These comprehension skills include: finding the main idea of a paragraph, noting related details, understanding how information is organized, and noting definitions and examples.

Every shorthand student aspires to be able to read fluently and without hesitation. When possible, students should read aloud assignments they have prepared for class, read the next assignment without previous preparation (this helps pinpoint potential difficulties), and read from homework notes. Since it's important that students become familiar with standard business vocabulary, practice material should be like that found in a local business office.

Students also need drill in basic dictionary skills, especially pronounciation and spelling skills.

Students should become familiar with a dictionary of shorthand outlines and a book of most commonly used words.

As a variation on textbook practice, make a shorthand game. Piercy(4) recommends two games: shorthand bingo and a shorthand cross-clue puzzle. In shorthand bingo, each student gets a card with 25 brief shorthand forms. A caller reads guide cards (B—great, G—state; N—morning). As discussed previously, the teacher can rely on advanced students to make the game boards and guide cards.

In the shorthand cross-clue puzzle, students read several paragraphs of text (which can be taken from a business letter or memo), noting that some words have been replaced with shorthand symbols. Puzzle placement is designated for each symbol (13 across, 4 down). Students try to solve the crossword puzzle by using the shorthand symbol or context clues from the text. Advanced classes might have all clues written in symbols. Students can check their accuracy from a key. This is another exercise that students can prepare under the direction of the teacher for extra credit. Both the bingo game and the crossword puzzle help students improve relevant vocabulary and spelling.

Nadler(5) recommends that teachers develop their own materials for supplementing textbook assignments. He uses biographies of famous Americans, counted off at the 1.4 level (14 syllables to 10 words). Students preview a list of difficult words before dictation begins.

General Nonskill Courses

Courses such as business law, general business, business organization, and economics generally require more reading of conventional text material than skill courses do. Generally students read this material for comprehension, rather than for directions. Students often encounter and complain about difficult vocabulary and difficult content.

In these classes reading for comprehension requires analysis and other higher level reading abilities. The course format generally requires reading for main ideas. Students tend to ignore the various reading aids incorporated into textbooks unless they are specifically directed to use them. These aids include questions at the beginning of each chapter, subheads, vocabulary guides and exercises, visuals with interpretive captions, case studies, and questions that follow sections or chapters.

Teachers should help students learn to skim material to get the main idea and learn to use subheads and chapter introductions and summaries. Once these pre-reading steps have been taken, the student can read the chapter with speed and comprehension. The teacher can improve the student's ability to handle these reading materials by preparing a study sheet for each new chapter. This study sheet might formulate chapter headings and subheads into questions students can think about as they read. For example: "What are negotiable instruments? How do they differ?" As students become familiar with this technique they will ask these questions on their own as they read.

Business Law

In business law textbooks, it is important to be familiar with the pattern of writing so one can know when to summarize ideas and when to go on to new ideas. Reading skills used in narrative material are simply not adequate. The pattern of writing in social studies is usually twofold: (1) presentation of a problem or situation, and (2) explanation of the problem or situation, sometimes with examples. In a business law text, however, the order is generally a bit more complex: (1) presentation of legal principle with concrete illustration or definition of main idea, (2) analysis of legal principles, and (3) solution to the problem. In business law the emphasis is on analysis rather than simple explanation.

Students often find it useful to skim the material, read it carefully, then restate the ideas in their own words. Class discussion can show students how to identify which legal principles apply, finally drawing a conclusion. The key issue here is that students need to spend more time clarifying their own explanations since the text doesn't provide much in the way of extensive explanations.

Another problem is new vocabulary. Some texts list new terms at the end of each chapter. Or the teacher can draw attention to and teach in context the meaning of some new words before the reading is assigned. Perhaps a team of students can scout out new, difficult words and provide relevant meanings for classmates. All students can be encouraged to notice and report how newly learned terms are used on television, in newspapers and magazines, and in other classes. With any approach the key is to avoid simple memorization of definitions; provide a meaningful context for each new word.

In business law, as in other areas of study, repetition will enhance student mastery of the material. Case studies, workbook exercises, and discussion of real-life applications will reinforce new ideas.

Because the business law textbook might be too difficult for some of the poor readers, advanced students might work together to rewrite the material in their own words. Rewritten material can be forwarded to typewriting classes. The job of producing meaningful, relevant, useful work will have positive effects all around.

SUMMARY

Students in business education classes are expected to read many different types of materials that demand a wide repertoire of reading strategies: skimming, proofreading, reading for comprehension, and reading directions. Reorganization of classroom time, activity, and resources can give business teachers more time to teach the variety of reading and business skills necessary for mastery of course material. It is vital that teachers see themselves as executives who orchestrate activity and delegate authority. This approach can free business education teachers to meet the wide variety of needs presented by a diverse student population and a broad range of subject areas and reading materials.

4. APPROPRIATE MATERIALS FOR BUSINESS EDUCATION

GENERAL GUIDELINES FOR MATERIALS SELECTION

It is the responsibility of every business education teacher to make sure that textbooks and supplementary materials provided for classes can be used successfully by the students. One of the teacher's chief roles in curriculum planning is the selection of appropriate teaching materials.

A good text is clearly organized and appealing enough to compete with similar stimuli the student encounters in related fields. Thus, a textbook must be evaluated first in relation to the students who will use it—their characteristics, their backgrounds, and the kinds of textbooks they are accustomed to reading. The text is a tool for learning, not a resource book for the teacher. First and foremost, it should communicate to the student.

Acceptable reading materials match or satisfy the objectives outlined for students in a particular school or a particular class. Thus, when judging a textbook, the teacher should have a clear idea of student needs and course goals. With needs and objectives in mind, a teacher can consider instructional and content values and format and utility.

The following list of questions should be helpful to business education teachers who are responsible for textbook evaluation:

Instructional Values

1. Do the materials fit the population? (consider reading level, concepts that match students' background, ways for students to work out problems presented by technical vocabulary)

2. Are instructional tasks arranged in an order that the student can follow? (consider clear objectives, frequent checkpoints, tasks the student can do independently)

3. Does the material lend itself to differentiated assignments and more than one level of learning? (consider subheads to help students, illustrations, balance between ideas and practice, pacing)

Content Values

4. Does the content cover most of the objectives for the course?

5. Does the content present social concerns in a reasonable manner? (look for a fair distribution of cultures and races, an absence of sex bias, and so forth)

6. Does the content include motivational and interest factors suitable to the age and culture of the population?

7. Does the content lead to a continuing interest and appreciation for the subject?

Format and Utility

8. Are the materials sufficiently attractive for their purpose? Are illustrations appealing to students? Is the type too small or too crowded?

9. Are different typographical techniques used to help the reader? (italics, boldface, variety of type sizes)

10. Are the materials easy to handle? (for example, will the typing textbook stay open while students do exercises?)

While the textbook is basic in each course, teachers should also take advantage of the other instructional opportunities that surround us in homes, supermarkets, drugstores, libraries, and so on. The problem is not a lack of material, but to select and gather appropriate material from that which is available. There is a wealth of supplementary materials available from publishers. Books, periodicals, newspapers, and government publications can also be used to supplement the textbook. Students can often help build a classroom library or provide sets of useful practice material. Supplementary materials are of critical importance in helping students learn independently.

READABILITY FORMULAS

How difficult are textbooks? Teachers often discuss the readability levels of various books. Although readability formulas are not the magic key to determining which book is appropriate for which student, these formulas can help teachers recognize possibilities or problems posed by particular texts or supplemental materials.

One way to measure the difficulty of reading material is by looking at sentence length and unfamiliar vocabulary. Other readability formulas look at sentence length and polysyllabic words. Others use semantic and syntactic complexity. Teachers must realize that no matter which formula is used, the formulas only attempt to quantify difficulty. No formula can measure student interest in the material, the purpose for reading it, or the student's previous experience with the concepts.

That is why the experience and personal judgment of the teacher are essential to any assessment of readability.

Taking these precautions into consideration, let's examine two simple formulas that measure word difficulty and sentence length. They each produce a rough estimate of readability with a minimum of work for the teacher.

The first formula, the Fog Index, involves four simple steps:

1. Take three 100-word passages—one from the beginning, one from the middle, and one from the end of the chapter or book.

2. Count how many words in each passage have three or more syllables. If the same three-syllable word appears several times, count it each time. Do not count proper names, compound words, or verb forms that become three syllables by adding -ed or -es.

3. Determine the average number of words per sentence in each passage—for example, 18 words per sentence. Record a partial sentence as, for example, 0.6 of a sentence.

4. Total factors 2 and 3 (the number of words of three or more syllables and the average sentence length), and multiply that sum by 0.4. The resulting figure is the Fog Index for that passage, represented in terms of the approximate grade level for which that passage is intended.

Robert Gunning(1), who developed the Fog Index, claims he found a good correlation between the Fog Index and the difficulty of writing. His sampling indicated popular magazines were written at these grade levels: *Atlantic Monthly*, 12; *Harper's*, 11; *Time*, 10; *Reader's Digest*, 9; *Ladies' Home Journal*, 8; and *True Confessions*, 7. The Fog Index is generally useful with more difficult prose material. It loses utility when the material is below the sixth grade level. Teachers should remember, however, that grade-equivalent numbers have only limited value in estimating readability because so many other factors contribute to reading difficulty: student experience and background with the topic, student interest and enthusiasm for the subject, the density of concepts in the text, and amount of inference the writer requires the reader to apply, etc. The score simply provides a bit of evidence to be coupled with other factors in deciding on the readability of a passage. The formula also makes objective comparisons among various passages a bit more convenient. The observant teacher uses the readability formula as a starting point for judging reading difficulty.

The Fry Graph(2) uses the same elements as the Fog Index for estimating readability. (Any discussion of readability should include measurement by at least two methods to show that estimates of difficulty vary from one formula to another.) The Fry Graph (see Appendix A, Text Reference VI) was developed as a quick, easy reference for estimating the reading difficulty of prose material, grade one through college. The graph determines difficulty on the basis of average sentence length and total number of syllables in a 100-word sample. The graph is limited, however, to passages of 108 to 172 syllables and those containing from 3.6 to 25 sentences.

Here is an example of some of the readability problems to which teachers need to become sensitive. A young child visits her mother's office and later writes about the experience:

> *There are files in the drawer. Mother can find what she needs. All the letters to Mr. Jones are in one place. Order forms are in another place.*

The child's mother, leaving instruction for a new office clerk, writes about the same filing system:

> *Correspondence is filed alphabetically and orders in numerical order.*

The differences between these passages help us understand the kinds of difficulties students encounter in their textbooks. The passage written by the young child presents one concept at a time, in concrete language, with only a minimum of inference required. The message unfolds sequentially, allowing the child time and mental space to grab hold of ideas and put them into recognizable order. Naturally, the sentences are short and the vocabulary is simple. The second statement makes assumptions about the mature reader. The writer assumes that the reader can compress ideas. The writer also assumes that the reader's background will enable the reader to fill in the details not explicitly provided. *Correspondence, alphabetically,* and *numerical* might not be understood by the child, but to the clerk they have specific meanings. The words *alphabetically* and *numerical* reflect abstract relationships that can be understood only after repeated concrete experiences with letter order and number order.

Another measure of reading difficulty is the "fistful of words" method. The teacher asks students in the class to read several passages silently and independently. As students read, they close a finger into their fist when they encounter a word they do not understand. Students record the number of difficult words (number of fingers) for each of the 100- to 200-word passages read. Two fists or ten difficult words indicate slow, frustrating reading. For this student, assignments should be modified, or different reading material should be used. The method is quick and informal, but it alerts the teacher to reading needs in a highly efficient way.

DEVELOPING AND FINDING MULTILEVEL MATERIALS

One way to solve the problem of readability is to involve students in writing texts. Classes with both advanced and slow students can rewrite portions of the textbook as a means of consolidating their own understanding. The brighter students can test out their revision on the slowest student to see what needs further clarification. In the process, the slowest students will be receiving individual attention from classmates as well as from the teacher.

One of the attractive values in the "write-your-own-text" approach is the combination of mature direction and student initiative. The reading-learning activity here is interactive, involving books and people. Students come to recognize the range of abilities in the group and the responsibility of each group to help its members succeed at varying levels. See Chapter 3 for tips on how to organize students for such projects.

As teachers gain experience with students and with materials, they develop more options and are better able to aid students. Students can help a beginning teacher build a file on available supplementary materials. The search for materials could result in a card file and a reference shelf filled with supplementary resource materials. Or beginners may want to try writing experimental study guides to help students at two or three different levels read and use a common text.

Too often a text is decided on by the administration and given to the teacher, who in turn hands it out to the student with the assumption that the student is now ready to start learning from it. The books are carted in, handed out, and the transaction has taken place. This approach encourages students to view textbooks as prefabricated parcels of knowledge. Rather than merely handing out the book, the teacher should give the students some orientation by discussing its virtues and limitations as a basis for learning.

If students cannot read a particular text, the most sensible thing to do is to find one with material they can read. There are books, magazines, pamphlets, and articles written at every reading level on almost every topic. Some publishers even specialize in producing mature books for students with a limited vocabulary. Each secondary school department usually has a budget for supplementary materials; library funds can be used to purchase some materials; home libraries and student scavenging can also serve learners.

For legitimate reasons, a teacher may want to use a single textbook with the whole class. In this case, the teacher can still differentiate reading assignments so that each student uses the book according to his or her capability. Some students can read for a full integrated discussion; some can read the headings and summary to get the main thrust and major concepts; others can search for a few specific details (perhaps found in the headings or in a specific graph or chart). Study guides can help each group. Developing these study guides takes effort, of course, and the use of differentiated study guides implies a classroom organized into identified groups.

OBTAINING MULTILEVEL MATERIALS

A number of textbook companies realize that not every student is a good reader, and consequently publish alternatives in the form of more readable textbooks and supplementary materials for less capable readers. For example, Fearon-Pitman publishes the *Pacemaker Vocational Readers*, which they describe as "realistic, career-oriented stories for students in grades 7-12 reading considerably below grade level." These books introduce 10 jobs such as supermarket stock clerk, janitor, and short-order cook—jobs that require little or no experience and little or no reading ability. The company also publishes high-interest, low-vocabulary textbooks and workbooks for typewriting; modern clerical practice, retail merchandising, and other business classes. The Gregg Division of McGraw-Hill also publishes some materials that might be useful for poor readers. Their series, *A Career in the Modern Office*, has four text-workbooks "specially written for students who want to train for clerical jobs but who are unsuccessful with conventional textbooks." Teachers should check with the companies that publish

their adopted textbooks and with other publishers to see what materials might be available, either to replace or to supplement the classroom text.

Many teachers have a limited budget to purchase supplementary materials, but believe their students need alternatives to the class textbook. This situation again provides an opportunity for students to take some responsibility for their learning and help each other. Students can write letters to local businesses requesting information. This requires that students compose a letter, type it, and proofread it. After so many attempts at typing practice letters that are never answered but simply copied from the textbook, students may find real correspondence both exciting and challenging. In this assignment, they leave the school world and become part of the working world. The extra bonus, of course, is that through their efforts new reading materials are sent to the classroom. Does the local bike shop have pamphlets on how to fix a flat tire or how to grease a bike? What material can car dealers provide about new models? What training do people need to get jobs in these businesses?

Students might also write letters to local businesses and industries to find out more about jobs that interest them. How does the work of a church secretary differ from the work of a legal secretary or a school secretary? How similar is the work of a bookkeeper in an auto parts store to the work of a department store bookkeeper? How does retailing clothes differ from retailing home appliances? Students can write to personnel departments for job descriptions and for copies of job applications. Students can look up addresses of businesses in the Yellow Pages. This will help reinforce some reading skills, including the ability to work independently and pay attention to detail. Guidance counselors are another source of information about careers in business. They can be asked to supply pamphlets and booklets about various careers. Local service clubs such as Kiwanis, Rotary, and Elks might also be sources of help. Members can provide materials about their businesses, or they might want to adopt a class as a service project. Just reading through the Yellow Pages can give students a better idea of the kinds of businesses—and jobs—available in the community. They might choose to research something they know nothing about—home computers, for example.

One teacher in Pennsylvania who uses this letter-writing activity requires that a rough draft of the letter be approved before the student types the finished copy. That way, she can ensure that students have checked spelling and are making a reasonable request. The letter and envelope must be typed perfectly before they can be mailed. Students may at first be uncomfortable with the freedom to write their own letters, but after a bit of practice, they enjoy the chance to find out about something that interests them.

Students can bring in copies of advertisements for local businesses, and these can be analyzed in class. For example, how do the ads for the tire stores differ? Is there any "fine print" in the ads? How can comparison shopping save consumers money?

Lack of money need not prohibit the use of varied reading materials. With a little initiative, any class can find supplemental information that will appeal to all types of readers.

SUMMARY

In order to be effective, materials selection for business education classes must incorporate a recognition of the wide spread of student reading abilities in any given classroom. This recognition implies two obligations:

1. Business teachers are obliged to select texts that can reach a maximum number of students.

2. Business teachers are obliged to understand what makes material easy or difficult to read, so that assignments can be modified and materials of varying levels of difficulty can be obtained.

APPENDIX A

TEXT REFERENCE I: READING SKILLS NECESSARY IN BUSINESS COURSES*

	Reading verbal problems	Relationships/Formulas	Reading pictures, graphs	Applying theory	Following directions	Researching	Drawing conclusions, Critical reading	Seeing organization	Supporting details	Noting main idea	Vocabulary: Special symbols	Vocabulary: General	Vocabulary: Technical	Using parts of book	Reading/Study technique	Reading for purpose
Bookkeeping I & II	X	X	X	X	X	X	X	X	X	X	X	X	X	X	X	X
Introduction to Business	X		X	X	X	X	X	X	X	X		X	X	X	X	X
Typewriting I					X			X	X	X		X	X	X	X	X
Shorthand I			X	X	X						X	X	X	X	X	X
Office Machines				X		X		X		X			X		X	X
Secretarial Practice		X	X	X	X	X	X	X	X	X		X	X	X	X	X
Retailing I			X	X	X	X	X	X	X	X	X	X	X	X	X	X
Business Law			X	X	X	X	X	X	X	X		X	X	X	X	X

*Source: Adapted from David L. Shepherd, *Comprehensive High School Reading Methods* (Columbus, Ohio: Charles E. Merrill Publishing Co., 1978), p. 307.

TEXT REFERENCE II: PREREQUISITE SKILLS CHECKLIST

Student Names	Text comprehension	Concentration	Graphs and Tables	Basic concepts	Rate of reading	Author's structure	Application	Main ideas	Index, Contents	Using context with vocabulary	Vocabulary	Directions
1.												
2.												
3.												
4.												
5.												
6.												
7.												
8.												
9.												
10.												
11.												

Definition of Terms

Text comprehension: General ability to understand the text

Concentration: Ability to attend to reading for 15+ minutes at a sitting

Graphs and Tables: Ability to use and interpret those that appear in the text

Basic concepts: Grasp of prerequisite general knowledge in that topic area

Rate of reading: Reading speed that allows student to complete typical reading assignments in a reasonable amount of time

Author's structure: Ability to predict from an author's cues and writing patterns that an important piece of information follows

Application: Ability to apply knowledge gained in reading

Main ideas: Ability to discriminate what is important from what is not in a given passage

Index, Contents: Ability to use these tools efficiently

Using context with vocabulary: Ability to determine the meaning of unknown words using context clues

Vocabulary: Previous knowledge of technical and specialized vocabulary

Directions: Ability to follow directions as written in textbook

TEXT REFERENCE III: SAMPLE TEXTBOOK INVENTORY QUESTIONS

Questions to test familiarity with parts of the book:

1.   In the glossary, what is the definition of *depreciate*?
2.   Using the index, tell on what page you can find out about *account balances.*
3.   In Chapter 11, what two kinds of transfer methods are explained? (Hint: Look at the boldface words.)

Questions to test vocabulary:

"The causes that may justify such action by the employer are disobedience, disloyalty, incompetency, fraud, and nonperformance of duties by the employee."

1.   In this sentence, "dis-" at the beginning of words means _____.
2.   When is the employer allowed to take an action, according to this sentence?

"The journal provides a business owner with a complete record of his daily business transactions."

3.   In this sentence, *journal* means _____.

"An employer is liable for any careless or wrongful acts (torts) committed by his employee while the employee is acting within the scope of his employment."

4.   In this sentence, *torts* means _____.

Questions to test comprehension:

"A trial balance is a listing of the titles of the accounts and their balances in the order in which the accounts appear in the ledger. All debit balances are entered in one column of the trial balance, and all credit balances are entered in another column. These balances are then added to make sure that the total of the debit balances equals the total of the credit balances."

1.   A trial balance has two columns: One is the _____ and the other is the _____.
2.   When you add the total of the debit balances, you should compare it to the _____ to see that they are equal.
3.   In the sample chart of accounts on page 83, an account numbered 401 would be an _____ account. (asset, owner's equity, income, expense)
4.   In the sample ledger (page 79), what is the step you should do after you pencil-foot the total debits? (This requires student to follow numbered directions printed below the sample page.)

Questions to test process:

1. If you read that 20 percent of your graduating class of 350 students plans to go to college, how many students plan to go to college? Which of these formulas will help you find out?

    a. $.20 \div 350 =$ c. $350 \div 20 =$

    b. $.20 \times 350 =$ d. $350 - 20 =$

2. Give students a simple question requiring calculations or a process. Rather than ask for the answer, ask for the steps necessary to solve the problem.

TEXT REFERENCE IV: STUDY SKILLS CHECKLIST

SETTING: *Where I Study*

	Yes	No	Some-times
1. I have a place set aside for studying.	___	___	___
2. I keep materials needed for studying at my place.	___	___	___
3. I have good lighting and a quiet atmosphere.	___	___	___
4. I can avoid distractions at my study place.	___	___	___
5. Others understand that I am not to be unnecessarily disturbed while studying.	___	___	___

SYSTEM: *How I Study*

	Yes	No	Some-times
1. I have what I need available before I begin studying and I organize myself for each task.	___	___	___
2. I plan ahead and schedule my study time.	___	___	___
3. I keep a calendar of assignments and tests for all classes.	___	___	___
4. I set specific purposes for each assignment.	___	___	___
5. I concentrate while I am working and plan short breaks for relaxation.	___	___	___
6. I reward myself after I have accomplished my study purposes.	___	___	___

TEXT REFERENCE V: STRANDING MODEL (Business Class)

Time	Monday	Tuesday	Wednesday	Thursday	Friday
0 min					
5 min		5-minute business vocabulary activity using special root words (1)			Quiz on week's root words (1)
10 min	Preview text chapter a. Make outline of main ideas. (2) b. Locate unknown words in chapter. Turn in with page identified. (1) and (2)	Groups must rapidly locate and define teacher's selection from yesterday's unknown words (contest). (1) and (2)	BEGIN BUSINESS INTEREST PROJECTS (Some students leave the room. Others stay to catch up on assignments.) (5)	BRIEF LAB (3) a. Analyze new warranties. (3) b. Identify loopholes. (4) c. Try to answer student-generated questions. (2) and (4) d. Use new vocabulary in write-up. (1)	GROUP CONTEST Students must use books to answer questions prepared by other groups. (2) and (4)
15 min					
20 min		Trade outlines for warranties—check to see what is missing. Teams graded as a unit. (3)			
25 min	Groups of two or three students develop 5 to 10 questions about text based on outline. Place on index cards. (2) and (4)				
30 min		Homework: Condense portion of an assigned chapter—one to two pages. (2)			
35 min				Homework: Read chapter with unanswered questions in mind. (2)	Teacher leads students through chapter, pointing out key areas of study for next week's test. (2)
40 min	Homework: Outline warranty—main points. (3)	Teacher has selected best questions from index cards. Appropriate students write questions on board. They are likely to be on unit test. (2)	In groups of five, students read each others' condensations to get an overview of the entire chapter. (2)		
45 min				Informal comments about progress of interest projects. (5)	
50 min	Read and select from alternatives for business interest project. (5)				
55 min					

Numbers in parentheses indicate which general goals (see pp. 24-25) are being fulfilled.

TEXT REFERENCE VI: FRY READABILITY GRAPH

GRAPH FOR ESTIMATING READABILITY
By Edward Fry, Rutgers University Reading Center, New Brunswick, New Jersey

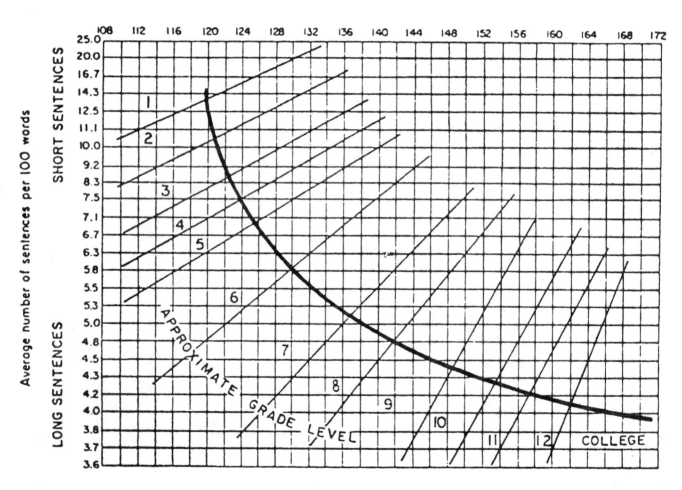

APPENDIX B

ANNOTATED BIBLIOGRAPHY OF MATERIALS ON READING IN BUSINESS EDUCATION CLASSES

Anderson, Bernice. "Business Teacher: Are You Prepared to Teach Reading?" *Business Education Forum* 26: 3-4; October 1971.

Business teachers should be able to develop their own skills in teaching students how to read textbooks and other course materials. Emphasizes the importance of analyzing materials to be used and how to help students study these materials.

Barbe, Walter B., and Swassing, Wayne. "Learning and Reading Disabilities." In *Learning Disabilities*. (John Clow and Ruth Woolschlager, editors.) Illinois Business Education Association, 1975.

One of five articles in this monograph, this examines the differences between learning and reading disabilities and suggests ways to help students with reading disabilities.

Becker, Herbert L. "Typewriting as a Tool for Improvement of Reading." *Typewriting Methods in the Seventies*, 28th Yearbook of the Business Education Association of Metropolitan New York, 1970, p. 104.

Suggests that typewriting offers a real opportunity to bring the senses of sight, hearing, and touch to bear on the problem of reading. For example, students' sight vocabulary increased by an inundation of thousands of quick repetitions and recreations of blends, words, phrase, and sentences. Typewriting also builds visual discrimination and attention to word details.

Foss, Florence. "Do Reading Scores Predict Typing Scores?" *Journal of Business Education* 41: 218-282; April 1966.

The faster the rate of reading, the speedier the typing performance in the beginning class, according to this study.

Hafner, Lawrence; Gualtney, Wayne; and Robinson, Richard. "Reading in Bookkeeping: Prediction and Performance." *Journal of Reading* 14: 537; May 1971.

Bookkeeping textbooks are heavily loaded with content, which makes them difficult to read.

Haggblade, Berle. "Using the Typewriter for Learning: Reading." *The Balance Sheet* 58: 106-110, 137; November 1979.

Maintaining that the typewriter is useful as a tool for corrective reading the author describes materials he used to increase word-recognition skills. These materials also helped improve word-level typing ability, thus advancing the course content.

Harrison, L. J. "Teaching Accounting Students How to Read." *Journal of Business Education* 35: 1969-1970; January 1960. Reprinted in Lawrence E. Hafner. *Improving Reading in Middle and Secondary Schools, Selected Readings*. New York: Macmillan, 1974. pp. 404-407.

When confronted with a class of students who had difficulty with assignments and exams, the author tried two procedures to improve student reading skills. Though he didn't want to sacrifice "accounting time" to "reading time," he concluded that with a little special effort business students can overcome special weaknesses.

House, F. Wayne. "Are You Solving the Reading Problem in Bookkeeping?" *Business Education World* 33: 291-292; February 1953.

House studied factors that affect student achievement in bookkeeping and found the density of technical terms heavy in early chapters of texts. The range of student reading ability is very wide. Thirty percent of the test questions based on early parts of the course were designed to measure the students' knowledge of technical terms.

Johnson, Verda R. "Teaching for Better Understanding in Typewriting." *Journal of Business Education* 41: 149-150; January 1966.

Although much of the reading done in typewriting classes is cursory, Johnson believes that reading can be incorporated into the classes. Her objectives are reading for content, reading to become word conscious, and reading with a research orientation.

Musselman, Vernon A. "The Reading Problem in Teaching Bookkeeping." *Business Education Forum* 14: 5-7; December 1959. Reprinted in Lawrence E. Hafner.

Improving Reading in Middle and Secondary Schools, Selected Readings. New York: Macmillan, 1974. pp. 398-404.

Several factors contribute to the heavy vocabulary load in bookkeeping, including common words with technical meanings and difficulty of materials. Musselman suggests six steps to overcome the problems, such as preparing vocabulary lists and using study guides as learning aids.

Nadler, Charles. "Supplemental Shorthand Reading Materials." *Journal of Business Education* 53: 223-226; February 1978.

A teacher can develop her own materials for a stimulating variation to the "bread and butter" letters and articles normally used in shorthand classes. Nadler suggests using other source materials that may interest students. He uses biographies and provides a preview list of words from the text. He counted off the material at the 1.4 m level (14 words to 10 syllables). A sample passage with preview list is included.

Nicoll, William. "Look/Learn." *Balance Sheet* 58: 161-165, 182; December 1976-January 1977.

The type size, type style, and layout of a typewriting textbook can play an important psychological role in learning.

Piercey, Dorothy. "Business." *Reading Activities in Content Areas.* Boston: Allyn and Bacon, 1976. pp. 55-71.

Activities in bookkeeping and shorthand classes can reinforce and teach reading skills. Piercey provides details and examples of several activities.

Reiff, Rosanne. "Recognizing a Major Problem in Business Education and Attempting to Solve It." *Balance Sheet* 56: 302-304; April 1975.

Poor reading ability is causing major problems in the teaching of business education. The author suggests ways to overcome this difficulty.

Robinson, H. Alan. "Additional Important Subjects: Business Courses." In *Teaching Reading and Study Strategies: The Content Areas.* Boston: Allyn and Bacon, 1975. pp. 211-216.

All teachers are able to guide students toward specialized books and periodicals that can whet appetites, improve performance, and help develop a lifetime reading habit. Bookkeeping, accounting, and business law textbooks are discussed here.

Robinson, Richard; Carter, John; and Hokanson, Don. "Business Teachers Are Reading Teachers." *Journal of Business Education* 44: 201-202; February 1969.

"Until business teachers, as well as other secondary instructors, fully realize their role in reading development, real progress will be hindered." Attitude of teachers is crucial to student success.

Schaefer, Julie C. and Paradis, Edward. "Help the Student with Low Reading Ability." *Journal of Business Education* 52: 160-162; January 1977.

Four techniques can help students with low reading abilities succeed in business education courses: establishing a purpose for reading, using the survey techniques, providing special interest projects, and adding supplementary reading materials in the classroom.

Shepherd, David. "Applying Reading Skills to Other Areas: Business Education." *Comprehensive H.S. Reading Methods.* Columbus, Ohio: Charles E. Merrill, 1973. pp. 277-282. Second edition, 1978; pp. 305-320.

Provides a list of classroom practices to enhance student reading skills and explains the SQ3R technique of reading for a business text.

Stewart, William D. "A Reading Approach to Shorthand Homework." *Journal of Business Education* 52: 268-270; March 1977.

Stewart describes a reading approach to shorthand homework in which students are graded on their in-class reading of the homework instead of being required to write the homework. A proposed grading scale and reading rates are included.

Strang, Ruth C., McCullough, and Traxler, M. "Special Reading Instruction Needed in Other Fields: Business Education." *The Improvement of Reading.* New York: McGraw-Hill, 1967. pp. 360-365.

The authors make brief suggestions for reading improvement in five business education classes.

Thomas, Ellen Lamar, and Robinson, H. Alan. "Typewriting and Business Education." *Improving Reading in Every Class.* Boston: Allyn and Bacon, 1977. pp. 343-353.

This chapter focuses on how to teach students to read

directions in typewriting texts more effectively, using examples from several textbooks. A student self-evaluation checklist is included.

Walters, George Lewis. "The Development and Refinement of Reading Skills in Business Education." Ed.D. dissertation, Northern Illinois University, 1973. Cincinnati: Southwestern Publishing Company, 1975. Monograph 128. 101 pp.

Wanous, S. J. "Typewriting as a Communication Skill." *Balance Sheet* 58: 57-59, 91; October 1976.

Students with poor reading skills misunderstand directions that accompany drills and problems. They also have problems with proofreading. Business teachers should help students improve communication skills.

REFERENCES

CHAPTER 1: RATIONALE FOR READING INSTRUCTION IN BUSINESS EDUCATION CLASSES

1. Leo Fay, "In Perspective," *Secondary Reading: Theory and Application* (Bloomington, Ind.: Monographs in Language and Reading Studies, School of Education, September 1978).

2. Kenneth Dulin, "The Middle Half: How Alike Are They, Really?" *Journal of Reading* 13: 603-609; May 1970.

3. Eugene Wyllie, Conversation with authors, Indiana University, November 21, 1978.

4. David Shepherd, "Applying Reading Skills to Other Areas: Business Education," in *Comprehensive High School Reading Methods*, 2nd ed. (Columbus, Ohio: Charles E. Merrill, 1978), pp. 305-320.

CHAPTER 2: ASSESSMENT TECHNIQUES

1. Henry Bamman, Ursula Hogan, and Charles Greene, *Reading Instruction in the Secondary Schools* (New York: Longmans, Green and Co., 1961).

2. John Bormuth, *Cloze Tests as Measures of Readability and Comprehension Ability*. Doctoral dissertation, Indiana University, 1962.

CHAPTER 3: ORGANIZING THE BUSINESS CLASSROOM AND STUDENTS FOR INSTRUCTION

1. F. Wayne House, *Factors Affecting Student Achievement in Beginning Bookkeeping in High School*. Doctoral dissertation, Ohio State University, 1951.

2. Vernon A. Musselman, "The Reading Problem in Teaching Bookkeeping," *Business Education Forum* 14: 5-7; December 1959.

3. F. Wayne House, "Are You Solving the Reading Problem in Bookkeeping?" *Business Education World* 33: 291-292; February 1953.

4. Dorothy Piercey, "Business," in *Reading Activities in Content Areas* (Boston: Allyn and Bacon, 1976), pp. 55-71.

5. Charles Nadler, "Supplemental Shorthand Reading Materials," *Journal of Business Education* 53: 223-226; February 1978.

CHAPTER 4: APPROPRIATE MATERIALS FOR BUSINESS EDUCATION

1. Robert Gunning, "The Fog Index After 20 Years," *Journal of Business Communication* 6: 3-13; Winter 1968.

2. Edward Fry, "Graph for Estimating Readability—Extended," *Journal of Reading* 21: 1; January 1977.